# THERE'S A DINOSAUR!

**Evelyn Stone**
**Illustrated with photographs**

HAMPTON-BROWN

## What are dinosaurs?

Dinosaurs are the biggest animals that ever lived on land. They lived a long, long time ago.

When dinosaurs lived on Earth, there were no people. In those days, dinosaurs ruled.

Many different kinds of dinosaurs lived together. A lot of them were very big, but some were very little. Some ate meat. Some ate plants. Some lived on land. Some lived in the sea.

Dinosaurs did what they wanted to do. They went where they wanted to go. There was no one to stop them!

Then all the dinosaurs died.
That is the truth.
Today you will not find one *living* dinosaur, but there are dinosaurs all around. You can see them—if you know where to look.

# Dinosaurs in Theme Parks

You might see a dinosaur in a theme park. These are fake dinosaurs, but they look real! They are made out of steel frames and plastic skin. Just look at the size of those teeth! But don't let them scare you. The teeth are fake, too, and these dinosaurs will not bite.

# Dinosaurs in Movies

Have you ever seen a dinosaur movie? The dinosaurs in movies are also fake, but they can look very real. They can be pretty scary, but that's all right. It's fun to be scared when it's just a movie.

8

# Dinosaurs in the Desert

A dinosaur walked on this desert a long time ago. You can see its prints in the dried mud. They look just like they did when the dinosaur was alive.

Dinosaur prints can tell us about the dinosaur that made them. They can tell us how big the dinosaur was. They can tell us how fast the dinosaur was running.

This is a dinosaur nest. It really is!
A dinosaur laid her eggs here. The
sun and the sand have made the
eggs as hard as rocks. It's sad to
think that these eggs will never hatch.

This is a dinosaur grave. A dinosaur died here. You can see its bones.

People dig dinosaur bones out of the earth. Then they put the bones back together with care to make a dinosaur skeleton.

# Dinosaurs in Museums

A museum is a great place to see a dinosaur. Dinosaur skeletons are on display there. Other displays may show what dinosaurs ate and where they laid their eggs. They show what the earth looked like when dinosaurs lived.

## Dinosaurs Everywhere

Keep looking and you will see a dinosaur.

Here is one in a sandbox. It must be Sandysaurus!

This dinosaur stands right in the middle of a highway.

Look! There's a dinosaur flying in the sky!

This dinosaur is in the dump.
How sad!

Wow! This dinosaur could scare your socks off!

Don't be afraid. He may look mean, but he's not. He isn't even real. All the *real* dinosaurs are gone, and maybe that's a good thing. Just think what life would be like if REAL dinosaurs still walked the earth!